D1626800

curries

simple and delicious easy-to-make recipes

MARKS &
SPENCER

Marks and Spencer p.l.c.
PO Box 3339,
Chester, CH99 9QS

shop online
www.marksandspencer.com

Copyright © Exclusive Editions 2006

All rights reserved. No part of this publication may be reproduced, stored in a retrieval system or transmitted, in any form or by any means, electronic, mechanical, photocopying, recording or otherwise, without the prior permission of the copyright holder.

ISBN: 1-84461-654-1

Printed in China

This edition designed by Talking Design, Worthing

The views expressed in this book are those of the author but they are general views only and readers are urged to consult a relevant and qualified specialist for individual advice in particular situations. Marks and Spencer p.l.c. and Exclusive Editions Limited hereby exclude all liability to the extent permitted by law for any errors or omissions in this book and for any loss, damage or expense (whether direct or indirect) suffered by a third party relying on any information contained in this book.

NOTES FOR THE READER

- This book uses both metric and imperial measurements. Follow the same units of measurement throughout; do not mix metric and imperial.
- All spoon measurements are level: teaspoons are assumed to be 5 ml, and tablespoons are assumed to be 15 ml.
- Unless otherwise stated, milk is assumed to be full fat, eggs and individual vegetables such as potatoes are medium, and pepper is freshly ground black pepper.
- Recipes using raw or very lightly cooked eggs should be avoided by infants, the elderly, pregnant women, convalescents and anyone suffering from an illness.
- Optional ingredients, variations or serving suggestions have not been included in the calculations.
- The times given are an approximate guide only. Preparation times differ according to the techniques used by different people and the cooking times vary as a result of the type of oven used.

contents

introduction

The word curry is derived from 'kari', meaning sauce, and was first used by the British in the eighteenth century to describe spicy Indian sauces served with rice. Soon after, those returning from service in the East India Company invented a British version of these Indian dishes, based on curry powder, something no Indian cook would countenance. Nowadays, with the upsurge in foreign travel, an increasingly multi-cultural society and a fascination with ethnic cooking, we have a much greater understanding of the careful balance and harmony of spices and other flavourings inherent in Indian cuisine.

Now that traditional ingredients, from dhal to garam masala, are available in supermarkets, it has never been easier to create authentic Indian curries and the recipes in this book provide the perfect guide. Of course, not all curries are Indian and you will also find mouthwatering Thai, Malaysian and other South East Asian dishes with their own unique piquancy and spice. Some are searingly hot, while others are more delicate and aromatic and the chapters feature in turn poultry and meat, fish and seafood, and vegetables. Finally, to create a real taste of Asia in your own kitchen, you will find a collection of irresistible accompaniments.

guide to recipe key

 CATEGORY

Recipes are graded as follows:
1 pea = easy, 2 peas = very easy, 3 peas = extremely easy.

 SERVES 4

Recipes generally serve four people. Simply halve the ingredients to serve two, taking care not to mix imperial and metric measurements.

 10 MINUTES

Preparation time.

 10 MINUTES

Cooking time.

poultry & meat

Whether your taste is for creamy and delicate Chicken Korma, fragrant and fresh-tasting Coconut Beef Curry or colourful and fiery Pork Vindaloo, you are sure to find the perfect spicy treat for you and your family among the recipes in this chapter. Even confirmed curry-lovers may be surprised by the sheer variety of dishes, with their wide range of ingredients, fascinating spectrum of spices, different cooking techniques and variable degrees of heat, all of which make them not just delicious and attractive meals to eat, but also an adventure and pleasure to prepare and cook.

chicken korma

1 chicken, weighing 1.3 kg/3 lb 225 g/8 oz ghee or butter 3 onions, thinly sliced 1 garlic clove, crushed 2.5-cm/1-inch piece fresh root ginger, grated	1 tsp mild chilli powder 1 tsp turmeric 1 tsp ground coriander ½ tsp ground cardamom ½ tsp ground cinnamon ½ tsp salt 1 tbsp gram flour 125 ml/4 fl oz milk	500 ml/18 fl oz double cream fresh coriander leaves, to garnish freshly cooked rice, to serve

Put the chicken into a large saucepan, cover with water and bring to the boil. Reduce the heat, cover and simmer for 30 minutes. Remove from the heat, lift out the chicken and set aside to cool. Reserve 125 ml/4 fl oz of the cooking liquid. Remove and discard the skin and bones. Cut the chicken into bite-sized pieces.

Heat the ghee in a large saucepan over a medium heat. Add the onions and garlic and cook, stirring, for 3 minutes, or until softened. Add the ginger, chilli powder, turmeric, ground coriander, cardamom, cinnamon and salt and cook for a further 5 minutes. Add the chicken and the reserved cooking liquid. Cook for 2 minutes.

Blend the flour with a little of the milk and add to the pan, then stir in the remaining milk. Bring to the boil, stirring, then reduce the heat, cover and simmer for 25 minutes. Stir in the cream, cover and simmer for a further 15 minutes.

Garnish with coriander leaves and serve with freshly cooked rice.

VERY EASY **SERVES 4 – 6** 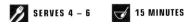 **15 MINUTES** **20 MINUTES**

chicken tikka masala

30 g/1 oz ghee or 2 tbsp
  vegetable or groundnut oil
1 large garlic clove, finely
  chopped
1 fresh red chilli,
  deseeded and chopped
2 tsp ground cumin
2 tsp ground paprika

½ tsp salt
black pepper
400 g/14 oz canned
  chopped tomatoes
300 ml/10 fl oz double
  cream
8 pieces shop-bought
  cooked tandoori chicken

fresh coriander sprigs,
  to garnish

To make the tikka masala, melt the ghee or heat the oil in a large frying pan with a lid over a medium heat. Add the garlic and chilli and stir-fry for 1 minute. Stir in the cumin, paprika, salt and pepper to taste and continue stirring for about 30 seconds.

Stir the tomatoes with their juices and the cream into the pan. Reduce the heat to low and leave the sauce to simmer for about 10 minutes, stirring frequently, until it reduces and thickens.

Meanwhile, remove all the bones and any skin from the tandoori chicken pieces, then cut the meat into bite-size pieces.

Adjust the seasoning of the sauce, if necessary. Add the chicken pieces to the pan, cover and leave to simmer for 3–5 minutes until the chicken is heated through. Sprinkle with the coriander to serve.

EASY   **SERVES 4**   **25 MINUTES** 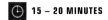 **15 – 20 MINUTES**

thai green chicken curry

2 tbsp groundnut or
  sunflower oil
500 g/1 lb 2 oz skinless
  boneless chicken
  breasts, cut into cubes
2 kaffir lime leaves,
  roughly torn
1 lemongrass stalk,
  finely chopped
225 ml/8 fl oz canned
  coconut milk

16 baby aubergines, halved
2 tbsp Thai fish sauce
fresh Thai basil sprigs,
  to garnish
kaffir lime leaves, thinly
  sliced, to garnish
GREEN CURRY PASTE
16 fresh green chillies
2 shallots, sliced
4 kaffir lime leaves
1 lemongrass stalk, chopped

2 garlic cloves, chopped
1 tsp cumin seeds
1 tsp coriander seeds
1 tbsp grated fresh root
  ginger or galangal
1 tsp grated lime rind
5 black peppercorns
1 tbsp sugar
salt
2 tbsp groundnut or
  sunflower oil

First make the curry paste. Deseed the chillies if you like and roughly chop. Place all the paste ingredients except the oil in a mortar and pound with a pestle. Alternatively, process in a food processor. Gradually blend in the oil.

Heat 2 tablespoons of oil in a preheated wok or large, heavy-based frying pan. Add 2 tablespoons of the curry paste and stir-fry briefly until all the aromas are released.

Add the chicken, lime leaves and lemongrass and stir-fry for 3–4 minutes, until the meat is beginning to colour. Add the coconut milk and aubergines and simmer gently for 8–10 minutes, or until tender.

Stir in the fish sauce and serve immediately, garnished with Thai basil sprigs and lime leaves. Reserve the remaining curry paste and keep in the refrigerator for future use.

lamb do piaza

4 onions, sliced into rings
3 garlic cloves,
   coarsely chopped
2.5-cm/1-inch piece fresh
   root ginger, grated
1 tsp ground coriander
1 tsp ground cumin
1 tsp chilli powder
½ tsp turmeric

1 tsp ground cinnamon
1 tsp garam masala
4 tbsp water
5 tbsp ghee or vegetable oil
600 g/1 lb 5 oz boneless
   lamb, cut into bite-sized
   chunks
6 tbsp natural yoghurt
salt

fresh coriander leaves,
   to garnish
freshly cooked rice,
   to serve

Put half of the onion rings into a food processor with the garlic, ginger, ground coriander, cumin, chilli powder, turmeric, cinnamon and garam masala. Add the water and process to a paste.

Heat 4 tablespoons of the ghee in a saucepan over a medium heat. Add the remaining onions and cook, stirring, for 3 minutes. Remove from the heat. Lift out the onions with a slotted spoon and set aside. Heat the remaining ghee in the pan over a high heat, add the lamb and cook, stirring, for 5 minutes. Lift out the meat and drain on kitchen paper. Add the onion paste to the pan and cook over a medium heat, stirring, until the oil separates. Stir in the yoghurt, season with salt to taste, return the lamb to the pan and stir well.

Bring the mixture gently to the boil, reduce the heat, cover and simmer for 25 minutes. Stir in the reserved onion rings and cook for a further 5 minutes. Remove from the heat, pile on to freshly cooked rice and garnish with coriander leaves. Serve immediately.

EASY **SERVES 4 – 6** **25 MINUTES +
2 HOURS
TO MARINATE** **1 HOUR**

lamb pasanda

600 g/1 lb 5 oz boneless
  lamb shoulder or leg
2 tbsp garlic and ginger
  paste (make by blending
  together equal quantities
  of fresh garlic and root
  ginger)
55 g/2 oz ghee or 4 tbsp
  vegetable or groundnut oil
3 large onions, chopped

1 fresh green chilli,
  deseeded and chopped
  (optional)
2 green cardamom pods,
  lightly crushed
1 cinnamon stick,
  broken in half
2 tsp ground coriander
1 tsp ground cumin
1 tsp ground turmeric

250 ml/9 fl oz water
150 ml/5 fl oz double
  cream
4 tbsp ground almonds
1½ tsp salt
1 tsp garam masala
paprika, to garnish
toasted flaked almonds,
  to garnish

Cut the meat into thin slices, then place the slices between clingfilm
and bash with a rolling pin or meat mallet to make them even thinner.
Put the lamb slices in a bowl, add the garlic and ginger paste and use
your hands to rub the paste into the lamb. Cover and set aside in a
cool place to marinate for 2 hours.

Melt the ghee in a flameproof casserole or large frying pan with a
tight-fitting lid over a medium-high heat. Add the onion and chilli, if using,
and fry, stirring frequently, for 5–8 minutes until the onion is golden brown.

Stir in the cardamom pods, cinnamon stick, coriander, cumin and turmeric
and continue stirring for 2 minutes, or until the spices are aromatic.

Add the meat to the pan and fry, stirring occasionally, for about 5 minutes
until it is brown on all sides and the fat begins to separate. Stir in the
water and bring to the boil, still stirring. Reduce the heat to its lowest
setting, cover the pan tightly and simmer for 40 minutes, or until the
meat is tender.

When the lamb is tender, stir the cream and almonds together in a bowl.
Beat in 6 tablespoons of the hot cooking liquid from the pan, then gradually
beat this mixture back into the casserole. Stir in the salt and garam masala.
Continue to simmer for a further 5 minutes, uncovered, stirring occasionally.

Garnish with a sprinkling of paprika and toasted flaked almonds to serve.

VERY EASY **SERVES 4** **20 MINUTES +
30 MINUTES
TO MARINATE**  **1 HOUR – 1 HOUR
10 MINUTES**

lamb rogan josh

350 ml/12 fl oz natural
  yoghurt
½ tsp ground asafoetida
  dissolved in 2 tbsp water
700 g/1 lb 9 oz boneless
  leg of lamb, trimmed
  and cut into 5-cm/2-inch
  cubes

2 tomatoes, deseeded
  and chopped
1 onion, chopped
30 g/1 oz ghee or 2 tbsp
  vegetable or groundnut oil
1½ tbsp garlic and ginger
  paste (see page 16)
2 tbsp tomato purée

2 bay leaves
1 tbsp ground coriander
¼–1 tsp chilli powder,
  ideally Kashmiri chilli
  powder
½ tsp ground turmeric
1 tsp salt
½ tsp garam masala

Put the yoghurt in a large bowl and stir in the dissolved asafoetida. Add
the lamb and use your hands to rub in all the yoghurt mixture, then set
aside for 30 minutes to marinate.

Meanwhile, put the tomatoes and onion in a blender and whiz until
blended. Melt the ghee in a flameproof casserole or large frying pan
with a tight-fitting lid. Add the garlic and ginger paste and stir around
until you can smell cooked garlic.

Stir in the tomato mixture, tomato purée, bay leaves, coriander, chilli
powder and turmeric, reduce the heat to low and simmer, stirring
occasionally, for 5–8 minutes.

Add the lamb and salt with any leftover marinade and stir around for
2 minutes. Cover, reduce the heat to low and simmer, stirring occasionally,
for 30 minutes. The lamb should give off enough moisture to prevent it
catching on the base of the pan, but if the sauce looks too dry, stir in a
little water.

Sprinkle the lamb with the garam masala, re-cover the pan and continue
simmering for 15–20 minutes until the lamb is tender when poked with
a fork. Adjust the seasoning, if necessary.

VERY EASY   **SERVES 4 – 6**   **20 MINUTES**   **1 HOUR 50 MINUTES**

beef madras

1–2 dried red chillies
2 tsp ground coriander
2 tsp ground turmeric
1 tsp black mustard seeds
½ tsp ground ginger
¼ tsp ground pepper
140 g/5 oz creamed
  coconut, grated and

dissolved in 300 ml/
  10 fl oz boiling water
55 g/2 oz ghee or 4 tbsp
  vegetable or groundnut oil
2 onions, chopped
3 large garlic cloves,
  chopped

700 g/1 lb 9 oz lean
  stewing steak, such as
  chuck, trimmed and cut
  into 5-cm/2-inch cubes
250 ml/9 fl oz beef stock
lemon juice
salt

Depending on how hot you want this dish to be, chop the chillies with or without any seeds. The more seeds you include, the hotter the dish will be. Put the chopped chilli and any seeds in a small bowl with the coriander, turmeric, mustard seeds, ginger and pepper and stir in a little of the coconut mixture to make a thin paste.

Melt the ghee in a flameproof casserole or large frying pan with a tight-fitting lid over a medium-high heat. Add the onions and garlic and fry for 5–8 minutes, stirring often, until the onion is golden brown. Add the spice paste and stir around for 2 minutes, or until you can smell the aromas.

Add the meat and stock and bring to the boil. Reduce the heat to its lowest level, cover tightly and simmer for 90 minutes, or until the beef is tender when you poke it with a fork. Check occasionally that the meat isn't catching on the base of the pan and stir in a little extra water or stock, if necessary.

Uncover the pan and stir in the remaining coconut milk with the lemon juice and salt to taste. Bring to the boil, stirring, then reduce the heat again and simmer, still uncovered, until the sauce reduces slightly.

balti beef curry

2 tbsp ghee or vegetable oil
1 onion, thinly sliced
1 garlic clove, finely
  chopped
3-cm/1¼-inch piece fresh
  root ginger, grated
2 fresh red chillies,
  deseeded and
  finely chopped

450 g/1 lb rump steak,
  cut into thin strips
1 green pepper, deseeded
  and thinly sliced
1 yellow pepper, deseeded
  and thinly sliced
1 tsp ground cumin
1 tbsp garam masala
4 tomatoes, chopped

2 tbsp lemon juice
1 tbsp water
salt
chopped fresh coriander,
  to garnish
Naan Bread, to serve

Heat half the ghee in a preheated wok or large, heavy-based frying pan. Add the onion and cook over a low heat, stirring occasionally, for 8–10 minutes, or until golden. Increase the heat to medium, add the garlic, ginger, chillies and steak and cook, stirring occasionally, for 5 minutes, or until the steak is browned all over. Remove with a slotted spoon, reserve and keep warm.

Add the remaining ghee to the wok, add the peppers and cook over a medium heat, stirring occasionally, for 4 minutes, or until softened. Stir in the cumin and garam masala and cook, stirring, for 1 minute.

Add the tomatoes, lemon juice and water, season with salt to taste and simmer, stirring constantly, for 3 minutes. Return the steak mixture to the wok and heat through. Serve immediately, garnished with chopped fresh coriander and accompanied by Naan Bread.

coconut beef curry

1 tbsp ground coriander
1 tbsp ground cumin
3 tbsp Mussaman Curry Paste
150 ml/¼ pint water
75 g/2¾ oz creamed coconut
450 g/1 lb beef fillet, cut into strips
400 ml/14 fl oz coconut milk
50 g/1¾ oz unsalted peanuts,
  chopped finely
2 tbsp fish sauce
1 tsp palm sugar or soft, light
  brown sugar
4 kaffir lime leaves
boiled rice with chopped fresh coriander,
  to serve

FOR THE MUSSAMAN CURRY PASTE
4 large dried red chillies
2 tsp shrimp paste
3 shallots, chopped finely
3 garlic cloves, chopped finely
2.5-cm/1-inch piece fresh galangal,
  chopped finely
2 lemongrass stalks (white part only),
  chopped finely
2 cloves
1 tbsp coriander seeds
1 tbsp cumin seeds
seeds from 3 cardamom pods
1 tsp black peppercorns
1 tsp salt

First make the curry paste. Cut off and discard the chilli stalks and place the chillies in a bowl. Cover with hot water and set aside to soak for 30–45 minutes. Wrap the shrimp paste in foil and grill or dry-fry for 2–3 minutes, turning once or twice. Remove from the grill or frying pan. Dry-fry the shallots, garlic, galangal, lemongrass, cloves, coriander, cumin and cardamom seeds over a low heat, stirring frequently, for 3–4 minutes, until lightly browned. Transfer to a food processor and process until finely ground. Add the chillies and their soaking water, peppercorns and salt, and process again. Add the shrimp paste and process again to a smooth paste, scraping down the sides as necessary.

Combine the coriander, cumin and curry paste in a bowl. Pour the measured water into a saucepan, add the creamed coconut and heat until it has dissolved. Add the curry paste mixture and simmer for 1 minute.

Add the beef and simmer for 6–8 minutes, then add the coconut milk, peanuts, fish sauce and sugar. Simmer gently for 15–20 minutes, until the meat is tender.

Add the lime leaves and simmer for 1–2 minutes. Serve the curry hot with rice with freshly chopped coriander stirred through it.

VERY EASY

 SERVES 4 – 6

 15 MINUTES +
20 MINUTES
TO COOL

 55 MINUTES –
1 HOUR
15 MINUTES

pork vindaloo

4 tbsp mustard oil
2 large onions, finely
  chopped
6 fresh bay leaves
6 cloves
6 garlic cloves, chopped
3 green cardamom pods,
  lightly cracked

1–2 small fresh red
  chillies, chopped
2 tbsp ground cumin
½ tsp salt
½ tsp ground turmeric
2 tbsp cider vinegar
2 tbsp water
1 tbsp tomato purée

700 g/1 lb 9 oz boneless
  shoulder of pork,
  trimmed and cut into
  5-cm/2-inch cubes

Put the mustard oil in a large frying pan or saucepan with a tight-fitting lid over a high heat until it smokes. Turn off the heat and leave the mustard oil to cool completely.

Reheat the oil over a medium-high heat. Add the onions and fry, stirring frequently, for 5–8 minutes until soft but not coloured.

Add the bay leaves, cloves, garlic, cardamom pods, chillies, cumin, salt, turmeric and 1 tablespoon of the vinegar to the onion and stir. Stir in the water, then cover the pan and simmer for about 1 minute, or until the water is absorbed and the fat separates.

Dissolve the tomato purée in the remaining tablespoon of vinegar, then stir it into the pan. Add the pork and stir.

Add just enough water to cover the pork and bring to the boil. Reduce the heat to its lowest level, cover the pan tightly and simmer for 40–60 minutes until the pork is tender.

If too much liquid remains in the pan when the pork is tender, use a slotted spoon to remove the pork from the pan and boil the liquid until it reduces to the required amount. Return the pork to heat through and adjust the seasoning, if necessary.

 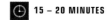
red curry pork with peppers

2 tbsp vegetable or
  groundnut oil
1 onion, roughly chopped
2 garlic cloves, chopped
450 g/1 lb pork fillet,
  sliced thickly
1 red pepper, deseeded
  and cut into squares

175 g/6 oz mushrooms,
  quartered
2 tbsp Thai red curry paste
115 g/4 oz creamed
  coconut, chopped
300 ml/½ pint pork or
  vegetable stock

2 tbsp Thai soy sauce
4 tomatoes, peeled,
  deseeded and chopped
handful of fresh coriander,
  chopped
boiled noodles or rice,
  to serve

Heat the oil in a wok or large frying pan and fry the onion and garlic for
1–2 minutes, until they are softened but not browned.

Add the pork slices and stir-fry for 2–3 minutes until browned all over.
Add the pepper, mushrooms and curry paste.

Dissolve the coconut in the hot stock and add to the wok with the soy
sauce. Bring to the boil and simmer for 4–5 minutes until the liquid has
reduced and thickened.

Add the tomatoes and coriander and cook for 1–2 minutes before serving
with noodles or rice.

fish &
seafood

The recipes in this chapter are fast, fun and literally a world away from the typical fish dishes of the West. They are a great way to encourage healthy eating and will be a sure-fire success for ringing the changes in the family's weekday menu. Rest assured – you won't have to buy expensive, unfamiliar and exotic fish to create a truly authentic flavour, whether it originates in the Bay of Bengal or the Gulf of Thailand. At the same time, fish and seafood curries are fabulous for informal entertaining, as they look wonderful, taste terrific, seem special and are quick and easy to cook.

VERY EASY **SERVES 4** **25 MINUTES** **20 MINUTES**

seafood laksa

200 g/7 oz live mussels, scrubbed and debearded
250 g/9 oz rice noodles
2 tbsp chilli oil
3 garlic cloves, chopped
3 spring onions, diagonally sliced
3 fresh green chillies, deseeded and chopped

1 tbsp chopped fresh lemongrass
1 tbsp Thai red curry paste
2 tsp ground cumin
450 ml/16 fl oz coconut milk
450 ml/16 fl oz fish stock or water

1 tbsp rice wine or sherry
1 tbsp soy sauce
150 g/5½ oz cod fillets, rinsed and cut into chunks
150 g/5½ oz raw prawns, peeled and deveined
4 whole tiger prawns, cooked, to garnish

Discard any mussels with broken shells or any that refuse to close when tapped. Put the remaining mussels into a saucepan with a little water over a high heat, cover and bring to the boil. Cook for 4 minutes, shaking the pan occasionally. Remove the mussels from the heat, drain and reserve, discarding any that remain closed.

Cook the noodles in a large saucepan of lightly salted boiling water for 2 minutes (check the packet instructions). Drain well, then divide between 4 soup bowls.

Heat the oil in a saucepan over a medium heat, add the garlic and spring onions and cook, stirring, for 4 minutes. Add the chillies, lemongrass, curry paste and cumin and cook, stirring, for a further 3 minutes. Stir in the coconut milk, fish stock, rice wine and soy sauce, bring to the boil, then reduce the heat, add the cod and mussels and cook for 3 minutes. Add the prawns and cook for 2 minutes. Pour over the noodles in the soup bowls. Garnish with tiger prawns and serve.

EASY　　 **SERVES 4**　　 **20 MINUTES +
1 – 1¹/₂ HOURS
TO MARINATE**　　 **4 MINUTES**

prawn masala

2 fresh red chillies,
 deseeded and chopped
2 garlic cloves, chopped
½ onion, chopped
2.5-cm/1-inch piece fresh
 root ginger, chopped
1 tsp turmeric
1 tsp ground cumin

1 tsp garam masala
½ tsp sugar
½ tsp freshly ground
 black pepper
300 ml/10 fl oz natural
 yoghurt
2 tbsp chopped fresh
 coriander

500 g/1 lb 2 oz raw tiger
 prawns, peeled and tails
 left intact
sprigs of fresh coriander,
 to garnish
lime wedges, to serve
Naan Bread, to serve

Put the chillies into a food processor with the garlic, onion, ginger, turmeric,
cumin, garam masala, sugar, pepper and yoghurt. Process until
smooth, then transfer to a large, shallow dish. Stir in the coriander.
Thread the prawns onto skewers, leaving a small space at either end.
Transfer them to the dish and turn in the mixture until thoroughly
coated. Cover with clingfilm and refrigerate for 1–1¹/₂ hours.

Remove from the refrigerator and arrange the skewers on a grill rack lined
with foil. Cook under a preheated medium grill, turning and basting with
the marinade, for 4 minutes, until sizzling and cooked through.

Garnish with coriander sprigs and serve with lime wedges and
Naan Bread.

goan-style seafood curry

3 tbsp vegetable or
  groundnut oil
1 tbsp black mustard seeds
12 fresh curry leaves or
  1 tbsp dried
6 shallots, finely chopped
1 garlic clove, crushed
1 tsp ground turmeric
½ tsp ground coriander

¼–½ tsp chilli powder
140 g/5 oz creamed
  coconut, grated and
  dissolved in 300 ml/
  10 fl oz boiling water
500 g/1 lb 2 oz skinless,
  boneless white fish,
  such as monkfish or
  cod, cut into large chunks

450 g/1 lb large raw
  prawns, peeled
  and deveined
finely grated rind and
  juice of 1 lime
salt
lime wedges, to serve

Heat the oil in a kadhai, wok or large frying pan over a high heat. Add the mustard seeds and stir them around for about 1 minute, or until they jump. Stir in the curry leaves.

Add the shallots and garlic and stir for about 5 minutes, or until the shallots are golden. Stir in the turmeric, coriander and chilli powder and continue stirring for about 30 seconds.

Add the dissolved creamed coconut. Bring to the boil, then reduce the heat to medium and stir for about 2 minutes.

Reduce the heat to low, add the fish and simmer for 1 minute, stirring the sauce over the fish and very gently stirring it around. Add the prawns and continue to simmer for 4–5 minutes longer until the fish flesh flakes easily and the prawns turn pink and curl.

Add half the lime juice, then taste and add more lime juice and salt to taste. Sprinkle with the lime rind and serve with lime wedges.

 **EXTREMELY EASY** **SERVES 4** **20 MINUTES** **15 MINUTES**

fish curry with rice noodles

2 tbsp vegetable or groundnut oil	225 g/8 oz salmon fillets, cut into cubes, each about 2.5 cm/1 inch	handful of fresh coriander, chopped
1 large onion, chopped	225 g/8 oz cod, cut into cubes, each about 2.5 cm/1 inch	1 tsp palm sugar or soft, light brown sugar
2 garlic cloves, chopped		1 tsp fish sauce
75 g/3 oz button mushrooms		115 g/4 oz rice noodles
225 g/8 oz monkfish, cut into cubes, each about 2.5 cm/1 inch	2 tbsp red curry paste	3 spring onions, chopped
	400 g/14 oz canned coconut milk	50 g/2 oz beansprouts
		few Thai basil leaves

Heat the oil in a wok or large frying pan and gently fry the onion, garlic and mushrooms until softened but not browned.

Add the fish, curry paste and coconut milk and bring gently to the boil. Simmer for 2–3 minutes before adding half of the coriander, the sugar and fish sauce. Keep warm.

Meanwhile, soak the noodles for 3–4 minutes (check the packet instructions) or until tender and drain well through a colander. Put the colander and noodles over a saucepan of simmering water. Add the spring onions, beansprouts and most of the basil and steam on top of the noodles for 1–2 minutes or until just wilted.

Pile the noodles onto warmed serving plates and top with the fish curry. Scatter the remaining coriander and basil over the top and serve immediately.

VERY EASY   **SERVES 4 – 6**   **20 MINUTES +**
45 MINUTES –
4 HOURS
15 MINUTES
TO MARINATE   **20 MINUTES**

balti fish curry

900 g/2 lb thick fish
  fillets, such as
  monkfish, grey mullet,
  cod or haddock, rinsed
  and cut into large chunks
2 bay leaves, torn
140 g/5 oz ghee or
  150 ml/5 fl oz vegetable
  or groundnut oil

2 large onions, chopped
½ tbsp salt
150 ml/5 fl oz water
chopped fresh coriander,
  to garnish

FOR THE MARINADE
½ tbsp garlic and ginger
  paste (see page 16)

1 fresh green chilli,
  deseeded and chopped
1 tsp ground coriander
1 tsp ground cumin
½ tsp ground turmeric
¼–½ tsp chilli powder
salt
1 tbsp water

To make the marinade, mix the garlic and ginger paste, green chilli, ground coriander, cumin, turmeric and chilli powder together with salt, to taste, in a large bowl. Gradually stir in the water to form a thin paste. Add the fish chunks and smear with the marinade. Tuck the bay leaves underneath and leave to marinate in the refrigerator for at least 30 minutes, or up to 4 hours.

When you are ready to cook the fish, remove from the refrigerator 15 minutes in advance. Melt the ghee in a kadhai, wok or large frying pan over a medium-high heat. Add the onion, sprinkle with the salt and fry, stirring frequently, for 8 minutes, or until it is very soft and golden.

Gently add the fish and bay leaves to the pan and stir in the water. Bring to the boil, then immediately reduce the heat and cook the fish for 4–5 minutes, spooning the sauce over the fish and carefully moving the chunks around, until they are cooked through and the flesh flakes easily. Adjust the seasoning, if necessary, sprinkle with coriander and serve.

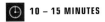
mixed seafood curry

1 tbsp vegetable or
   groundnut oil
3 shallots, chopped finely
2.5-cm/1-inch piece fresh
   galangal, peeled and
   sliced thinly
2 garlic cloves,
   chopped finely
400 ml/14 fl oz canned
   coconut milk

2 lemongrass stalks,
   snapped in half
4 tbsp fish sauce
2 tbsp chilli sauce
225 g/8 oz uncooked tiger
   prawns, peeled
225 g/8 oz baby squid,
   cleaned and sliced thickly
225 g/8 oz salmon fillet,
   skinned and cut into
   chunks

175 g/6 oz tuna steak,
   cut into chunks
225 g/8 oz fresh mussels,
   scrubbed and debearded
fresh Chinese chives,
   to garnish
boiled rice, to serve

Heat the oil in a large wok and stir-fry the shallots, galangal and garlic for
1–2 minutes, until they start to soften. Add the coconut milk, lemongrass,
fish sauce and chilli sauce. Bring to the boil, lower the heat and simmer
for 1–2 minutes.

Add the prawns, squid, salmon and tuna and simmer for 3–4 minutes,
until the prawns have turned pink and the fish is cooked.

Meanwhile, check through the mussels, discarding any with broken
shells or with open shells that refuse to close when tapped. Add the
mussels to the wok and cover with a lid. Simmer for 1–2 minutes,
until they have opened. Discard any mussels that remain closed.
Garnish with Chinese chives and serve immediately with rice.

vegetable
dishes

For both cultural and religious reasons, vegetarians are often
the rule rather than the exception in many parts of India
and South East Asia, so it should be no surprise to anyone
that vegetable curries are so varied and tasty. As well as
substantial curries that may simply be served with rice as
a main dish, there are recipes for side dishes, snacks and
appetizers. However you serve them and whether they feature
pulses or potatoes, onions or spinach, these vegetable
dishes are among the most versatile, imaginative and
inviting in the world.

VERY EASY   **SERVES 4**   **20 MINUTES**   **45 MINUTES**

vegetable korma

4 tbsp ghee or vegetable oil
2 onions, chopped
2 garlic cloves, chopped
1 fresh red chilli, chopped
1 tbsp grated fresh
  root ginger
2 tomatoes, peeled
  and chopped
1 orange pepper, deseeded
  and cut into small pieces

1 large potato,
  cut into chunks
200 g/7 oz cauliflower
  florets
½ tsp salt
1 tsp turmeric
1 tsp ground cumin
1 tsp ground coriander
1 tsp garam masala

200 ml/7 fl oz vegetable
  stock or water
150 ml/5 fl oz natural
  yoghurt
150 ml/5 fl oz single cream
25 g/1 oz fresh coriander,
  chopped
freshly cooked rice,
  to serve

Heat the ghee in a large saucepan over a medium heat, add the onions and garlic and cook, stirring, for 3 minutes. Add the chilli and ginger and cook for a further 4 minutes. Add the tomatoes, pepper, potato, cauliflower, salt and spices and cook, stirring, for a further 3 minutes. Stir in the stock and bring to the boil. Reduce the heat and simmer for 25 minutes.

Stir in the yoghurt and cream and cook, stirring, for a further 5 minutes. Add the fresh coriander and heat through.

Serve with freshly cooked rice.

courgette & cashew nut curry

2 tbsp vegetable or
  groundnut oil
6 spring onions, chopped
2 garlic cloves, chopped
2 fresh green chillies,
  deseeded and chopped

450 g/1 lb courgettes,
  cut into thick slices
115 g/4 oz shiitake
  mushrooms, halved
50 g/2 oz beansprouts
75 g/3 oz cashew nuts,
  toasted or dry-fried

few Chinese chives,
  chopped
4 tbsp Thai soy sauce
1 tsp fish sauce
rice or noodles, to serve

Heat the oil in a wok or large frying pan and fry the spring onions, garlic and chillies for 1–2 minutes, until softened but not browned.

Add the courgettes and mushrooms and cook for 2–3 minutes until tender.

Add the beansprouts, nuts, chives and both sauces and stir-fry for 1–2 minutes.

Serve hot with rice or noodles.

chickpeas with spiced tomatoes

6 tbsp vegetable or
  groundnut oil
2 tsp cumin seeds
3 large onions, finely
  chopped
2 tsp garlic and ginger
  paste (see page 16)
2 small fresh green
  chillies, deseeded and
  thinly sliced

1½ tsp ground mango
  (amchoor powder)
1½ tsp garam masala
¾ tsp ground asafoetida
½ tsp ground turmeric
¼–1 tsp chilli powder
3 large, firm tomatoes,
  about 450 g/1 lb, grated

800 g/1 lb 12 oz canned
  chickpeas, rinsed and
  drained
6 tbsp water
300 g/10½ oz fresh
  spinach leaves, rinsed
½ tsp salt

Heat the oil in a kadhai, wok or large frying pan over a medium-high heat. Add the cumin seeds and stir around for 30 seconds or until they brown and crackle, watching carefully because they can burn quickly.

Immediately stir in the onions, garlic and ginger paste and chillies and fry, stirring frequently, for 5–8 minutes until the onions are golden.

Stir in the ground mango, garam masala, asafoetida, turmeric and chilli powder. Add the tomatoes to the pan, stir them around and continue frying, stirring frequently, until the sauce blends together and starts to brown slightly.

Stir in the chickpeas and water and bring to the boil. Reduce the heat to very low and use a wooden spoon or a potato masher to mash about a quarter of the chickpeas, leaving the others whole.

Add the spinach to the pan with just the water clinging to the leaves and stir around until it wilts and is cooked. Stir in the salt, then taste and adjust the seasoning, if necessary.

sweet-and-sour lentils

250 g/9 oz split yellow
 lentils (chana dal)
1.2 litres/2 pints water
2 bay leaves, torn
3 fresh chillies, sliced
 once, but left whole
½ tsp ground turmeric
½ tsp ground asafoetida
3 tbsp vegetable or
 groundnut oil
½ onion, finely chopped

2-cm/¾-inch piece of
 fresh root ginger,
 finely chopped
30 g/1 oz creamed
 coconut, grated
1 fresh green chilli,
 deseeded or not,
 to taste, and chopped
1½ tbsp sugar
1½ tbsp tamarind paste
½ tsp garam masala

¼ tsp ground cumin
¼ tsp ground coriander
salt

TO GARNISH
15 g/½ oz ghee, melted,
 or 1 tbsp vegetable or
 groundnut oil
1 tsp garam masala
chopped fresh coriander

Put the lentils and water in a large saucepan with a lid over a high heat and bring to the boil, skimming the surface as necessary. When the foam stops rising, stir in the bay leaves, chillies, turmeric and asafoetida. Half-cover the pan and leave the lentils to continue simmering for about 40 minutes, or until they are very tender, but not reduced to a mush, and all the liquid has been absorbed.

When the lentils are almost tender, heat the oil in a kadhai, wok or large frying pan over a medium-high heat. Add the onion and ginger and fry, stirring frequently, for 5–8 minutes.

Stir in the coconut, green chilli, sugar, tamarind paste, garam masala, ground cumin and ground coriander and stir around for about 1 minute.

When the lentils are tender, add them, the bay leaves, chillies and any liquid left in the saucepan to the spice mixture and stir around to blend together. Taste and add salt, if necessary, and extra sugar and tamarind, if desired.

Transfer the lentils to a serving dish and drizzle the hot ghee over the top. Sprinkle with garam masala and coriander.

VERY EASY   **SERVES 4**   **15 MINUTES**   **40 MINUTES**

sag aloo

550 g/1 lb 4 oz frozen
  spinach
6 tbsp ghee or vegetable oil
1 onion, sliced
2 garlic cloves, chopped
2.5-cm/1-inch piece fresh
  root ginger, finely sliced

1 fresh red chilli, chopped
1 tsp turmeric
½ tsp paprika
250 g/9 oz potatoes,
  coarsely chopped
250 g/9 oz sweet
  potatoes, coarsely
  chopped

4 tbsp water
salt and pepper

Bring a saucepan of water to the boil, add the spinach and return to
the boil. Reduce the heat to medium and cook for 3 minutes. Drain
and refresh under cold running water. Squeeze out any excess water
from the spinach, then chop and set aside.

Heat the ghee in a large saucepan over a medium heat, add the onion
and garlic and cook, stirring, for 2 minutes. Add the spinach and the
remaining ingredients and bring to a simmer, then reduce the heat and
cover. Continue to simmer for 30 minutes, or until the potatoes are tender,
stirring occasionally and adding a little more water when necessary.

Remove from the heat and serve immediately.

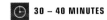
aloo gobi

55 g/2 oz ghee or 4 tbsp
  vegetable or groundnut oil
½ tbsp cumin seeds
1 onion, chopped
4-cm/1½-inch piece of
  fresh root ginger, finely
  chopped

1 fresh green chilli,
  deseeded and thinly sliced
450 g/1 lb cauliflower,
  cut into small florets
450 g/1 lb large waxy
  potatoes, peeled and
  cut into large chunks

½ tsp ground coriander
½ tsp garam masala
¼ tsp salt
fresh coriander sprigs,
  to garnish

Melt the ghee in a flameproof casserole or large frying pan with a tight-fitting lid over a medium-high heat. Add the cumin seeds and stir around for about 30 seconds until they crackle and start to brown.

Immediately stir in the onion, ginger and chilli and stir for 5–8 minutes until the onion is golden.

Stir in the cauliflower and potato, followed by the coriander, garam masala and salt, to taste, and continue stirring for about 30 seconds longer.

Cover the pan, reduce the heat to the lowest setting and simmer, stirring occasionally, for 20–30 minutes until the vegetables are tender when pierced with the point of a knife. Check occasionally that they aren't sticking to the base of the pan and stir in a little water, if necessary.

Taste and adjust the seasoning, if necessary, and sprinkle with the coriander to serve.

matar paneer

85 g/3 oz ghee or 6 tbsp
   vegetable or groundnut oil
350 g/12 oz paneer,
   cut into 1-cm/½-inch
   pieces
2 large garlic cloves,
   chopped

1-cm/½-inch piece of
   fresh root ginger,
   finely chopped
1 large onion, finely sliced
1 tsp ground turmeric
1 tsp garam masala
¼–½ tsp chilli powder

350 g/12 oz frozen peas
   or 600 g/1 lb 5 oz fresh
   peas, shelled
1 fresh bay leaf
½ tsp salt
125 ml/4 fl oz water
chopped fresh coriander,
   to garnish

Heat the ghee in a large frying pan or flameproof casserole with a tight-fitting lid over a medium-high heat. Add as many paneer pieces as will fit in a single layer without overcrowding the pan and fry for about 5 minutes until golden brown on all sides. Use a slotted spoon to remove the paneer and drain on crumpled kitchen paper. Continue, adding a little extra ghee, if necessary, until all the paneer is fried.

Reheat the pan with the ghee. Stir in the garlic, ginger and onion and fry, stirring frequently, for 5–8 minutes until the onion is soft, but not brown.

Stir in the turmeric, garam masala and chilli powder and fry for a further 2 minutes.

Add the peas, bay leaf and salt, to taste, to the pan and stir around. Pour in the water and bring to the boil. Reduce the heat to very low, then cover and simmer for 10 minutes, or until the peas are tender.

Gently return the paneer to the pan. Simmer, stirring gently, until the paneer is heated through. Taste and adjust the seasoning, if necessary. Sprinkle with coriander and serve.

onion bhaji

140 g/5 oz besan or
  gram flour
1 tsp salt
1 tsp ground cumin
1 tsp ground turmeric
1 tsp bicarbonate of soda

½ tsp chilli powder
2 tsp lemon juice
2 tbsp vegetable or
  groundnut oil, plus extra
  for deep-frying
2–8 tbsp water

2 onions, thinly sliced
2 tsp coriander seeds,
  lightly crushed
lemon wedges, to serve

Sift the besan flour, salt, cumin, turmeric, bicarbonate of soda and chilli powder into a large bowl. Add the lemon juice and the oil, then very gradually stir in just enough water until a batter similar to single cream forms. Mix in the onions and coriander seeds.

Heat enough oil for deep-frying in a kadhai, wok, deep-fat fryer or large, heavy-based saucepan until it reaches 180°C/350°F, or until a cube of bread browns in 30 seconds. Without overcrowding the pan, drop in spoonfuls of the onion mixture and fry for 2 minutes, then use tongs to flip the bhajis over and continue frying for a further 2 minutes, or until golden brown.

Immediately remove the bhajis from the oil and drain well on crumpled kitchen paper. Keep the bhajis warm while you continue frying the remaining batter. Serve hot with lemon wedges.

EASY MAKES 12  20–25 MINUTES + 15 MINUTES TO COOL 30 MINUTES

vegetarian samosas

FILLING
1 medium carrot, diced
200 g/7 oz sweet potato, diced
85 g/3 oz frozen peas
2 tbsp ghee or vegetable oil
1 onion, chopped
1 garlic clove, chopped

2.5-cm/1-inch piece fresh root ginger, grated
1 tsp turmeric
1 tsp ground cumin
½ tsp chilli powder
½ tsp garam masala
1 tsp lime juice
salt and pepper

PASTRY
150 g/5½ oz plain flour, plus extra for dusting
3 tbsp butter, diced
4 tbsp warm milk

vegetable oil, for frying
lime wedges, to serve
Mango Chutney, to serve

Bring a saucepan of water to the boil, add the carrot and cook for 4 minutes. Add the sweet potato and cook for 4 minutes, then add the peas and cook for 3 minutes. Drain. Heat the ghee in a saucepan over a medium heat, add the onion, garlic, ginger, spices and lime juice and cook, stirring, for 3 minutes. Add the vegetables and season. Cook, stirring, for 2 minutes. Remove from the heat and leave to cool for 15 minutes.

Put the flour into a bowl and rub in the butter. Add the milk and mix to form a dough. Knead briefly and divide into 4. On a lightly floured work surface, roll into balls, then roll out into circles 17 cm/6½ inches in diameter. Halve each circle, divide the filling between them and brush the edges with water, then fold over into triangles and seal the edges. Heat 2.5 cm/1 inch of oil in a frying pan to 190°C/375°F, or until a cube of bread browns in 30 seconds. Cook the samosas in batches for 3–4 minutes, or until golden. Drain on kitchen paper and serve with lime wedges and Mango Chutney.

accompaniments

The final touch of authenticity – and also part of the joy
of experimenting with foreign cooking – is to get the
accompaniments right. Perfect rice is a must with curries,
but there is also something immensely satisfying about
making your own chutney, raita and Indian breads, even
though you can buy these in a supermarket. All are easier
to make than you probably realize and some, such as chapatis,
are really quick. The only problem is that home-made
accompaniments are incredibly moreish so you may well
find yourself having to cook a second batch.

spiced basmati rice

225 g/8 oz basmati rice
30 g/1 oz ghee or 2 tbsp
  vegetable or groundnut oil
5 green cardamom pods,
  lightly cracked
5 cloves

2 bay leaves
½ cinnamon stick
1 tsp fennel seeds
½ tsp black mustard
  seeds
450 ml/16 fl oz water

1½ tsp salt
2 tbsp chopped fresh
  coriander
pepper

Rinse the basmati rice in several changes of water until the water runs clear, then leave to soak for 30 minutes. Drain and set aside until ready to cook.

Melt the ghee in a flameproof casserole or large saucepan with a tight-fitting lid over a medium-high heat. Add the spices and stir for 30 seconds. Stir the rice into the casserole so the grains are coated with ghee. Stir in the water and salt and bring to the boil.

Reduce the heat to as low as possible and cover the casserole tightly. Simmer, without lifting the lid, for 8–10 minutes until the grains are tender and all the liquid is absorbed.

Turn off the heat and use 2 forks to mix in the coriander. Adjust the seasoning, if necessary. Re-cover the pan and leave to stand for 5 minutes.

VERY EASY   **MAKES 10**  **20 MINUTES + 1¹/₂ HOURS TO REST** 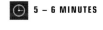 **5 – 6 MINUTES**

naan bread

900 g/2 lb strong
  white flour
1 tbsp baking powder
1 tsp sugar

1 tsp salt
300 ml/10 fl oz water,
  heated to 50°C/122°F
1 egg, beaten

55 g/2 oz ghee, melted,
  plus a little extra for
  rolling out and brushing

Sift the flour, baking powder, sugar and salt into a large mixing bowl and make a well in the centre. Mix together the water and egg, beating until the egg breaks up and is blended with the liquid.

Slowly add the liquid mixture to the well in the dry ingredients, using your fingers to draw in the flour from the side, until a stiff, heavy dough forms. Shape the dough into a ball and return it to the bowl.

Soak a clean tea towel in hot water, then wring it out and use it to cover the bowl, tucking the ends of the towel under the bowl. Set the bowl aside to let the dough rest for 30 minutes.

Turn out the dough on to a work surface brushed with melted ghee and flatten the dough. Gradually sprinkle the dough with the melted ghee and knead to work it in, little by little, until it is completely incorporated. Shape the dough into 10 equal balls.

Resoak the towel in hot water and wring it out again, then place it over the dough balls and leave them to rest and rise for 1 hour.

Meanwhile, put 1 or 2 baking sheets in the oven and preheat the oven to 230°C/450°F/Gas Mark 8 or its highest setting.

Use a lightly greased rolling pin to roll the dough balls into teardrop shapes, about 3 mm/¹/₈ inch thick. Use crumpled kitchen paper to lightly rub the hot baking sheets with ghee. Arrange the naans on the baking sheets and bake for 5–6 minutes until they are golden brown and lightly puffed. As you take the naans out of the oven, brush with melted ghee and serve at once.

chapatis

225 g/8 oz wholemeal flour, sifted,
 plus extra for dusting
½ tsp salt
150–200 ml/5–7 fl oz water
melted ghee, for brushing

Mix the flour and salt together in a large bowl and make a well in the centre. Gradually stir in enough water to make a stiff dough.

Turn out the dough on to a lightly floured surface and knead for 10 minutes, or until it is smooth and elastic. Shape the dough into a ball and place it in the cleaned bowl, then cover with a damp tea towel and leave to rest for 20 minutes.

Divide the dough into 6 equal pieces. Lightly flour your hands and roll each piece of dough into a ball. Meanwhile, heat a large, ungreased tava, frying pan or griddle over a high heat until very hot and a splash of water 'dances' when it hits the surface.

Working with 1 ball of dough at a time, flatten the dough between your palms, then roll it out on a lightly floured work surface into an 18-cm/ 7-inch round. Slap the dough on to the hot pan and cook until brown flecks appear on the bottom. Flip the dough over and repeat on the other side.

Flip the dough over again and use a bunched-up tea towel to press down all around the edge. This pushes the steam in the chapati around, causing the chapati to puff up. Continue cooking until the bottom is golden brown, then flip over and repeat this step on the other side.

Brush the chapati with melted ghee and serve, then repeat with the remaining dough balls. Chapatis are best served at once, as soon as they come out of the pan, but they can be kept warm wrapped in foil for about 20 minutes.

EXTREMELY EASY  **SERVES 4 – 6** **15 MINUTES** **0 MINUTES**

raita

1 large piece of cucumber, about 300 g/10½ oz, rinsed	½ teaspoon sugar
1 teaspoon salt	pinch of ground cumin
400 ml/14 fl oz natural yoghurt	2 tablespoons chopped fresh coriander or mint
	chilli powder, to garnish

Lay a clean tea towel flat on the work surface. Coarsely grate the unpeeled cucumber directly on to the towel. Sprinkle with ½ teaspoon of the salt, then gather up the towel and squeeze until all the excess moisture is removed from the cucumber.

Put the yoghurt into a bowl and beat in the remaining ½ teaspoon of salt, along with the sugar and cumin. Stir in the grated cucumber. Taste and add extra seasoning, if you like. Cover and chill until ready to serve.

Stir in the chopped coriander and transfer to a serving bowl. Sprinkle with chilli powder and serve.

VERY EASY  **MAKES ABOUT 250 G/9 OZ**  **20 MINUTES + 3 DAYS TO CHILL** **15 MINUTES**

mango chutney

1 large mango, about
   400 g/14 oz, peeled,
   stoned and finely chopped
2 tbsp lime juice
1 tbsp vegetable or
   groundnut oil
2 shallots, finely chopped

1 garlic clove, finely
   chopped
2 fresh green chillies,
   deseeded and finely
   sliced
1 tsp black mustard
   seeds

1 tsp coriander seeds
5 tbsp grated jaggery or
   light brown sugar
5 tbsp white wine vinegar
1 tsp salt
pinch of ground ginger

Put the mango in a non-metallic bowl with the lime juice and set aside.

Heat the oil in a large frying pan or saucepan over a medium-high heat. Add the shallots and fry for 3 minutes. Add the garlic and chillies and stir for a further 2 minutes, or until the shallots are soft, but not brown. Add the mustard and coriander seeds and then stir.

Add the mango to the pan with the jaggery, vinegar, salt and ground ginger and stir. Reduce the heat to its lowest setting and simmer for 10 minutes until the liquid thickens and the mango becomes sticky.

Remove from the heat and leave to cool completely. Transfer to an airtight container, cover and chill for 3 days before using. Store in the refrigerator and use within 1 week.

VERY EASY **MAKES
225 G/8 OZ**  **10 MINUTES +
19 – 23 DAYS
TO STAND** **5 MINUTES**

lime pickle

12 limes, halved and deseeded	25 g/1 oz mustard powder	300 ml/10 fl oz mustard oil
115 g/4 oz salt	25 g/1 oz ground fenugreek	15 g/½ oz yellow mustard seeds, crushed
70 g/2½ oz chilli powder	1 tbsp ground turmeric	½ tsp asafoetida

Cut each lime half into 4 pieces and pack them into a large sterilized jar, sprinkling over the salt at the same time. Cover and leave to stand in a warm place for 10–14 days, or until the limes have turned brown and softened.

Mix the chilli powder, mustard powder, fenugreek and turmeric together in a small bowl and add to the jar of limes. Stir to mix, then re-cover and leave to stand for 2 days.

Transfer the lime mixture to a heatproof bowl. Heat the mustard oil in a heavy-based frying pan. Add the mustard seeds and asafoetida and cook, stirring constantly, until the oil is very hot and just beginning to smoke. Pour the oil and spices over the limes and mix well. Cover and leave to cool. When cool, pack into a sterilized jar, seal and store in a sunny place for 1 week before serving.

EXTREMELY EASY   MAKES ABOUT   10 MINUTES +   0 MINUTES
                  225 G/8 OZ   15 MINUTES
                                     TO STAND/CHILL

chilli and onion chutney

1–2 fresh green chillies,
  deseeded or not, to
  taste, and finely chopped
1 small fresh bird's eye
  chilli, deseeded or not,
  to taste, and finely
  chopped

1 tbsp white wine or
  cider vinegar
2 onions, finely chopped
2 tbsp fresh lemon juice
1 tbsp sugar

3 tbsp chopped fresh
  coriander, mint or parsley,
  or a combination of herbs
salt
chilli flower, to garnish

Put the chillies in a small non-metallic bowl with the vinegar, stir around
and then drain. Return the chillies to the bowl and stir in the onions,
lemon juice, sugar and herbs, then add salt to taste.

Leave to stand at room temperature or cover and chill for 15 minutes.
Garnish with the chilli flower before serving.

index